STRESS FREE

BIG - BOLD - EASY COLORING BOOK

for All Ages

By Sharp Pen Publishing

Test Your Colors

Before you start coloring with markers, place a protective sheet behind the page to prevent bleed-through.

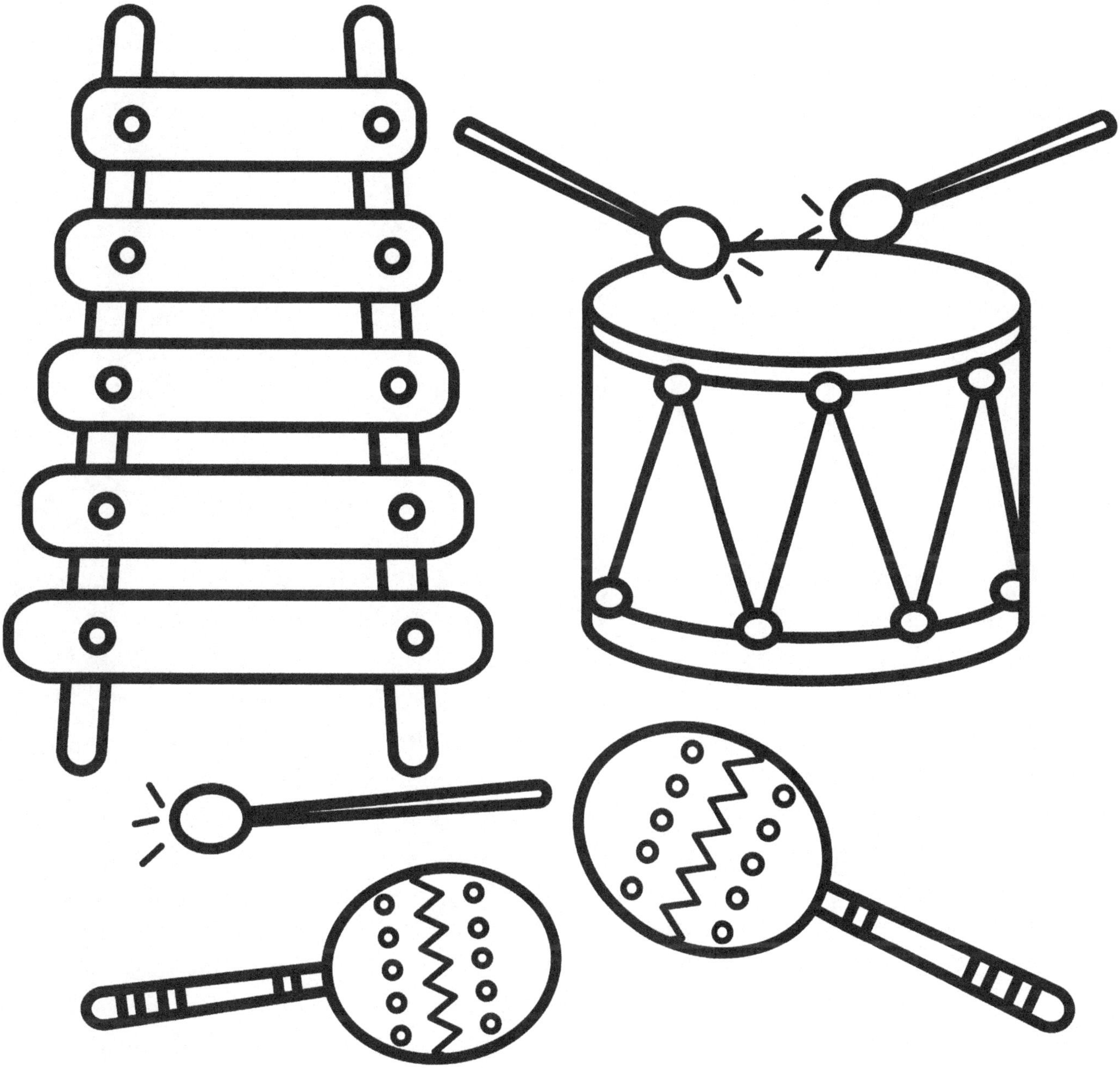

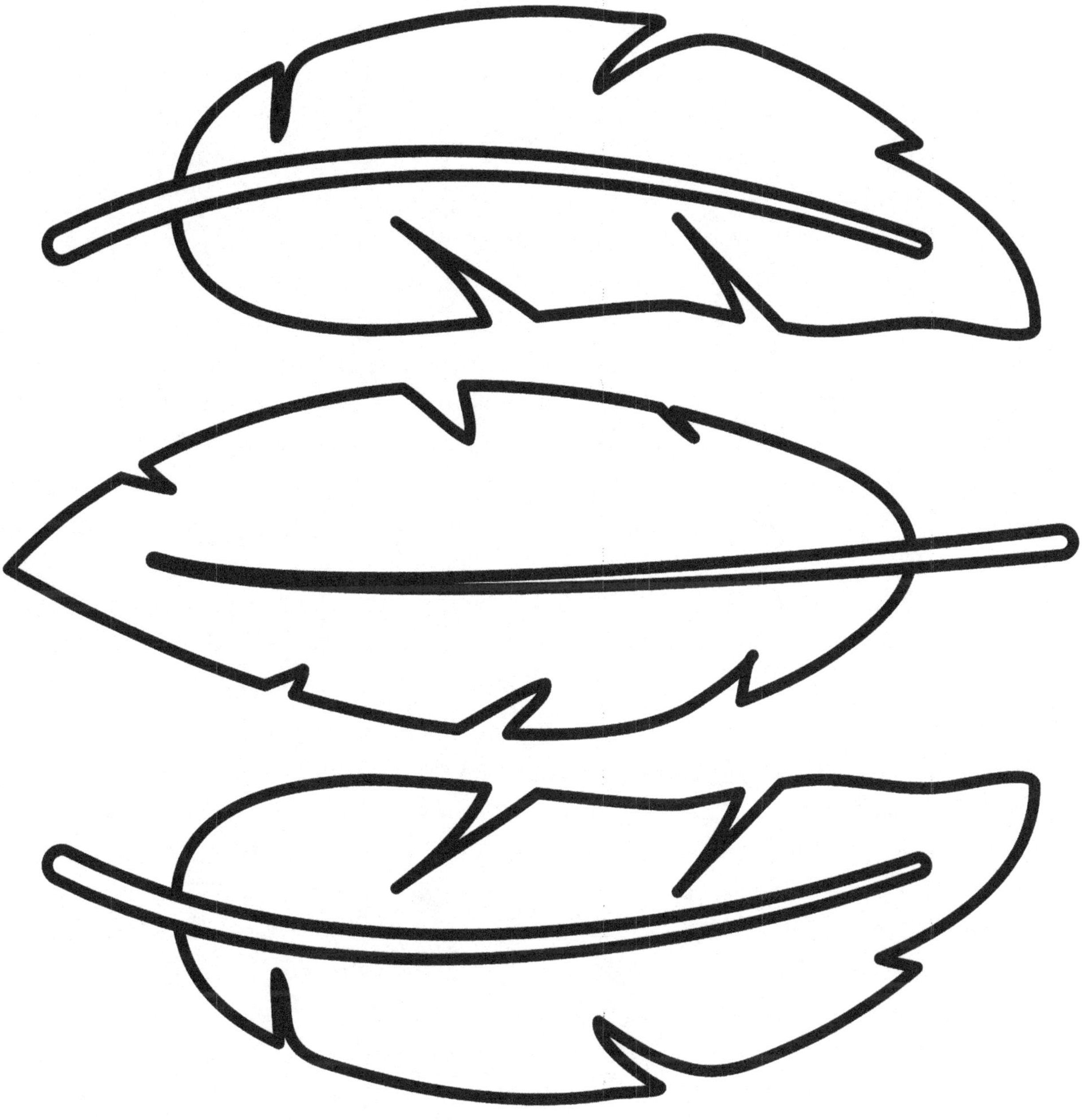

Z Z Z

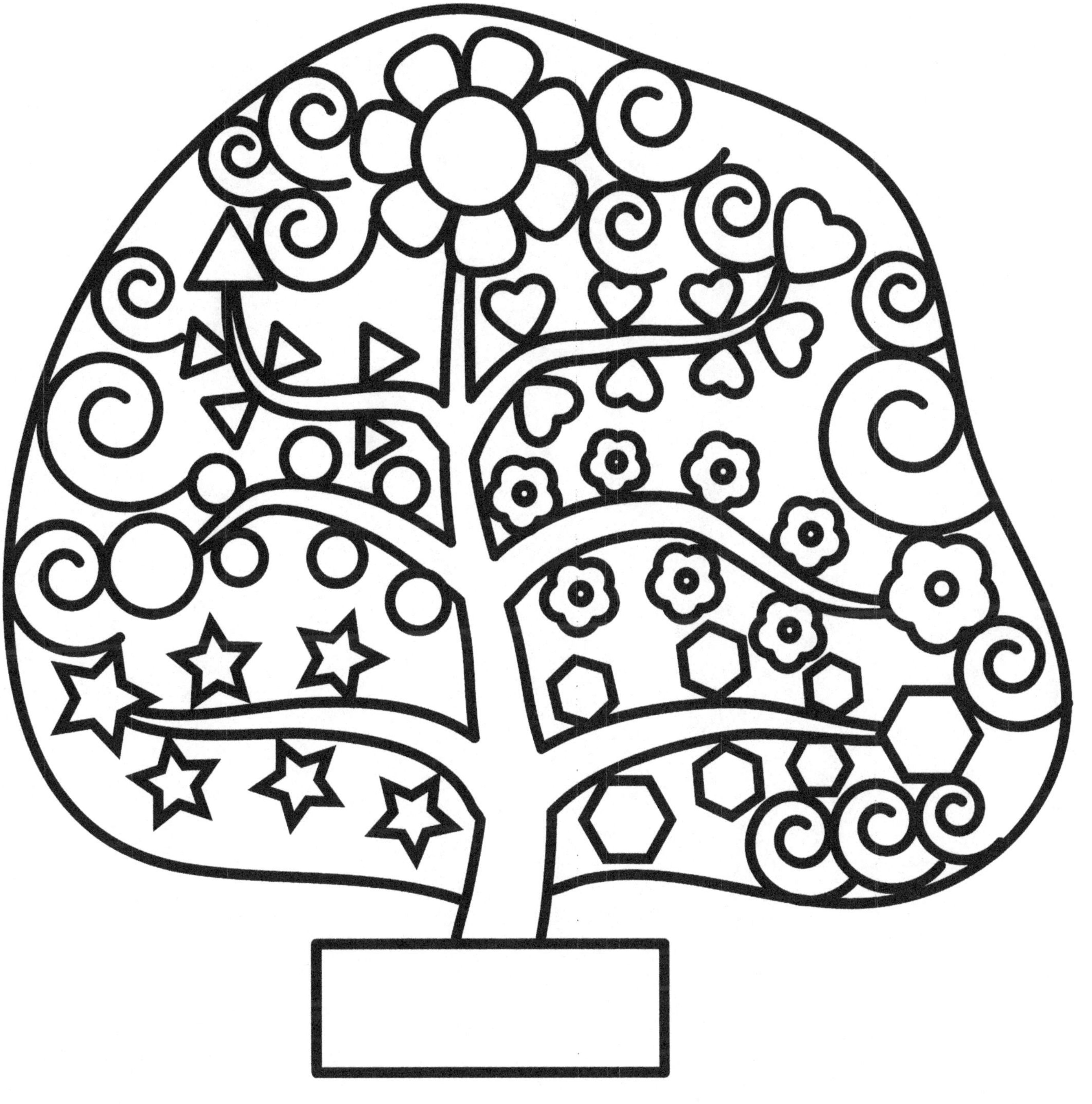

SUPER!

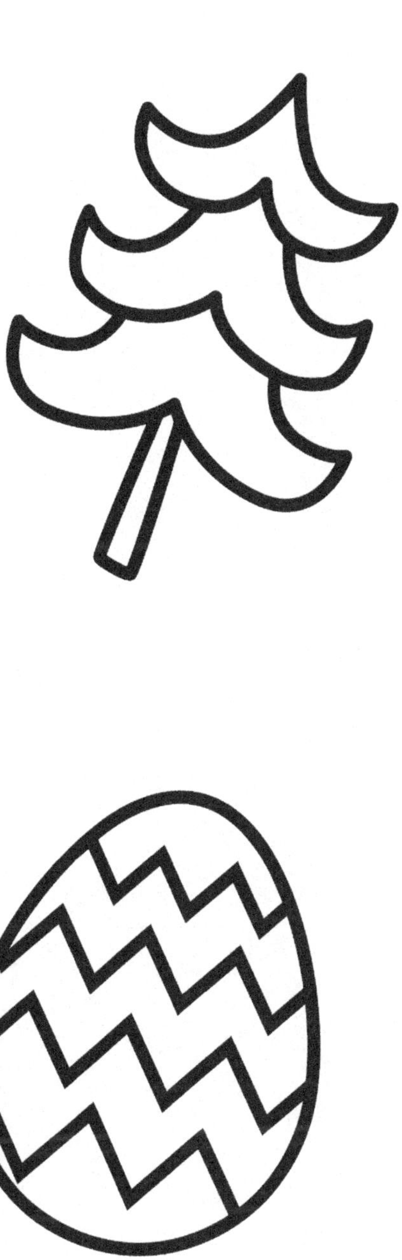

Thank You

Thank you for your purchase! If you enjoyed this book, please consider leaving a review. It takes 5 seconds and helps small businesses like ours.

Made in the USA
Las Vegas, NV
16 July 2024

92391350R00059